Crossing the Energetic doors

towards the meeting with the NAGUAL

Alicia Bauer

English translation by Danila Scialpi

Images: wanderer awake jones web orig

Introductory note to the English version:

There is a terminology, a specific language of the Toltec shamanism, that the author of the book uses in her Spanish language. In the English translation I have preferred to leave the terms in the original language "voladores", "nagual" and "ensueño", since in the translation they would have lost their pregnant meaning.

Particularly I refer to the original words "ensueño, ensoñador, ensoñar" as they intend a different state of conscience from "sueño" (dream); in English they have been translated with dream, dreamer, to dream, to give more fluency to the reading, nevertheless they point out that type of lucid dream.
D.S.

My thanks go to the forces which lead my destiny...

"I have already given myself to the power that governs my destiny.
I don't grab to anything anymore, so that I will not have anything to defend.

I don't have thoughts, so that I can see.

I am not afraid of anything, so that I can remember myself.

Serene and detached,
The Eagle will let me go towards freedom."

Don Juan Mattus, book: The silent knowledge.

Index

The crystals of power: practical techniques to be applied

The fire and the "voladores": practical techniques to be applied

The doors of lucid dream (ensueño)

The man or woman Nagual and the attentions

The Crystals of Power (Memories of the Pleiades)

There is an engine power, more powerful than steam, than electricity and than atomic energy: Will.

Albert Einstein

In our physical body energies, which we are not aware of, sail.
We study the anatomy, the physics, the chemistry of the human body, but nobody tells us of the thin forces that live into us and of their work. Among these, saved from the forgetfulness, is the science that has been left there in inheritance by the Pleiades through the atlantes:

The energies of Crystals in our physical body.

Like the earth is covered by telluric lines and it can or cannot unite in a point called " of power" so it happens to our physical body.

On the earth surface places abound where, for their particular position, forces are introduced that meet from different parts, forging them of some properties; the man who experiences that is unable to explain what makes it special, he succeeds only in saying: this place has something magic. This "magic" is the strength of the energies that cross channels which, like routes, we call telluric, and that meet in a certain physical point equipping it with power.

Properties of crystals:

-they open energetic doors to other planes of our conscience, according to their position in our body, it will be the place where they transport us.

- they allow us to travel through channels, as tunnel of worms, towards separate planes, dimensions from which we can take the knowledge in them, and in applying that knowledge to our daily life we can reach the evolution of our soul as well as a life full of adventures, going out of the collective conscience.

-to contact teachers of different dimensions receiving direct education without intermediaries.

-to increase our average of life completing with awareness the task for which we were born, with joy, succeeding in leaving aside the pre-concepts of sacrifice.

-the possibility to re-write our book of life, changing our destiny.

-to balance the terrestrial and celestial forces in our physical body (the power to turn oneself into a wayfarer between the sky and the earth).

-to re-clean the strings that we have with the soul and the original source.

-to recover the power of the energy of fire (life) inside us in such a way to be as living torches.

-to succeed in reaching our original place as children of the sun.

- to incorporate in conscious form the legitimate power of the ray and the light that comes with it.

-to recover the true sense of love without conditions experimenting it in our daily life. (Visiting the world of fairies and of unicorns).

And even more...

Place of way out or physical expression of the crystallized energy:

in a woman: the median point between her two ovaries; in a man: the middle point between his two testicles.
-the middle point in the low abdomen.
-the middle point two (2) fingers under the navel.
-solar plexus, about four or five fingers above the navel.
-the middle point of the breast
-the middle point among the eyebrows.
-crown.

Activation of crystals

The energies that cross our body don't find a point of exit for their expression, because of different blocks that are materialized in it through our thoughts, fears, emotions, beliefs, physical and/or emotional pains.
Therefore the first thing to do is to balance the terrestrial and celestial energies inside us so that they will equip us with the necessary strengths to free the physical blocks of these energies.

A lot of illnesses of the body manifest themselves through these blocks, it happens when we have a psychosomatic reaction to them, we transform a psychic affection into an organic one.
When we allow with our will and firm intention that everything stopping the exit of the energies, which unite themselves in those points, flows towards the outside of our physical body, with more strength and naturalness the energies of the physical centres of power will flow and will manifest themselves in our daily reality.

All of this will allow us to perceive a lot beyond what, until now, our physical eyes see and at the same time to heal many of our illnesses, both physical and emotional, giving us the possibility to connect us with all the potential of ours.

The practical exercises that are described below must be experimented not only through the mind, but also with the body. It is of primary importance to experiment with the body to leave aside any doubt regarding if it is a game of our mind or our imagination.

1- Practical exercise of terrestrial and celestial balance:
   "Being like a tree".

The ideal thing is to do this exercise remaining still and with your feet a bit separated from one another to have a certain balance.

a -Start visualizing that from one of the plants of our feet roots grow that sink in the depth of the earth as far as reaching the nucleus of fire that lives in its inside.

b- Do the same thing with the other foot and when its roots are in the centre of the earth, unite these roots in the same point with the roots of the other foot.
(In the case of women, visualize that from their vagina roots are born that sink in the earth down to its centre uniting themselves in the same point with the roots of their feet).

Explanation: men: two roots; women: three roots.

c - In the centre of the earth the fire giver of life lives, make this fire climb up for each of the roots, reach our feet, and keep on directing it upward, crossing our body inside to go out through the crown and from there reach the sky.
This exercise must be done "feeling" with our body the rising of the fire and the visualization of how it invades all of our physical inside.

d - From the sky and with our will, make the celestial energies (colour blue-silver) lower, make them come down through our crown, make them cross all the inside of our body, up to reach the roots and, from there, the earth centre. This exercise is to be done in the same way of the previous one: "feeling" with our body and visualizing.

For the beginners, it is recommended to repeat the exercises "c and d", ten times a day.

It is possible that in the course of the balance of both the forces in our physical body, various symptoms happen, to be known: nauseas, indispositions, tickling, warm, cold, etc. These symptoms are products of our unbalance and with the practice they will go re-balancing.

For those people who have already been practicing for various weeks, it is recommended to do three daily sessions of the exercises: c and d.

Always, at the end of the sessions, keep again the roots in our inside, withdrawing them with our will until they remain again inside us.

This exercise helps us to gather again the lost energy in those blocks, assembling it in the centres of power that are in our physical body.

2 - Practical exercise to unblock every centre of power.

    a- Start visualizing an opening or a hole that is in one of the centres above mentioned, with our will and intention push so that everything living there and stopping the exit of the energies goes out of us. Feel with your body what goes out, it doesn't matter what, and, if possible, visualize it. Continue with this cleaning, until at the end we feel and perceive a constant flow of a pale-coloured energy that gushes out from that centre.

b - With our will "crystallize" that energy, make it solid as crystal. You will feel and see like a long crystalline stick that emerges from our physical body toward the outside.
This stick has its "seat" in our inside and it extends out of it.
    c- Once already crystallized that energy and always with the use of our will, "we will activate it" making it turn on itself and in the same place.
    d- Repeating the points: a, b and c, we will go and unblock each one of the centres of power and crystallize those energies for their following use.

3 - Possible uses of crystals

I use the word "possible" in the uses that can be given to these crystals of power, because I will detail some roughly and not everyone; every person in their own practice and experience will find a broadening, change and/or other uses of them.

a - Every time that a crystal must be used, it must return to "to emerge", "to expand" towards the outside of our body, without losing its base in us. If you make it turn as hands of clock it will quickly produce an energetic opening, an " energetic door" that connects us to a pipe as a tunnel of worms; this tunnel will bring us to other planes of conscience, to other worlds.
It depends from where we want to go (direction) and for what reason (intention) the choice of the crystal that we use or the combination of crystals that we use.

We always need an intention and a direction. We will perceive this energetic door as a circle of energy and if we pay the due attention, we will see the entrance to that tunnel in its centre.

I must highlight some points to keep in mind not "to lose ourselves" in our trip with a simple and daily example:

If I decide to go out and go to the bakery (direction) to buy some bread (intention) and during the journey I become distracted with a neighbour chatting with him, then I observe how the house in the corner is being built, and later something recalls my attention in the kiosk of magazines, I will NEVER reach the bakery and, finally I won't buy the bread.

In the path that we are crossing there will always be something that distract us from our destination, and here we must pay a lot of attention... it is important not to let us attract from what we see on the sides of the road, not everything is what seems to be, we require a constant and impeccable ambush or in other words: not everything that shines is gold. We can lose ourselves in labyrinths from which we will not always know to go out.

b - to combine at the same time various crystals, you are not asked to make them turn as hands of clock, the only union of their points will produce an explosion of energy that will open an energetic door, to which we will already have given direction and intention.

Example: if I want to unite the points of the crystal which is under the navel with the one in the centre of the breast to that of the forehead, I leave the crystal of the breast straight and I give the necessary inclination to the other two so that they unite to the middle one.
All is done through our will and intention.

The daily practice will increase our energetic capability, which will allow us to travel towards different planes of conscience, worlds and dimensions, where we will find teachers that live in those places and from whom we will receive their knowledge; applying that knowledge in our daily life, in ourselves, in our relationships with the others, will lead us to the evolution of our soul. It will make us understand and know how our individual conscience is formed, the collective conscience and how to go out of that collective conscience in which we feel caught.

c - Fundamental functions (not necessarily the only ones) of every crystal:

Crystal of the gonads: it awakens, increases and raises the sexual energy. The explanation of the use of that energy deserves a book apart, but it is enough to know for the time being that energy is not only for having sexual relationships or to generate children, the saving of the same one can be used as "fuel" to dream (ensoñar), among other things. Many know it as "kundalini", "sacred tantra", etc.

Crystal of the low abdomen: bowels in men, matrix (uterus) in women, centre of great storing of cumulative energy, with its correspondent creative power.

Crystal under the navel or tan-tiem: the centre of the spirit in us and our direct relationship with:
The Great Spirit, Intent, God, Universal Energy, or as you want to call it.

Crystal of the solar plexus: the place where the base of our human and social relationships, like the self-imposed obstacles, low self-esteem, etc. This centre is mostly connected with our mental part, since our emotions (not the feelings) are produced in it.

Crystal of the centre of the breast: base of the energy of unconditional love, it is usually blocked, we succeed only in having human feelings of attachment.

Crystal of the eyebrow: energetic base of clairvoyance, visualization, base of "general command", mental power.

Crystal of the crown: energetic base of the union of the stellar energies.

There are other centres of energetic power and not all meet in the known chakras, neither all meet in the human body. However the same constant job inside oneself will bring to find them and to situate them, according to the personal evolution of each of us.

Examples picture 1 and 2

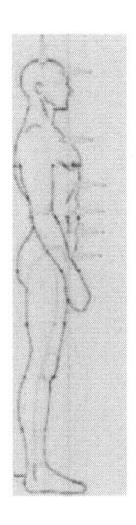

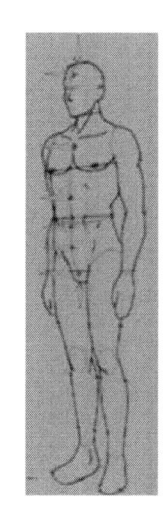

Children of the Sun

Once the crystals have emerged and activated in front of our physical body, make the conscious extension of the same ones towards the back.

With our will and high intention extend the crystals until you make them emerge from our shoulder, one by one, as the crown one emerges upward, extend it until that it crosses us from north to south or vice versa.

Once this extension has been done, practise daily the turning (activation) of the crystals altogether, at the same time and with the same speed. Let's gradually increase that speed up to reach a maximum speed of ignition while we spy what is happening on the points of every crystal in the performing of this exercise, and what happens with our physical body in this ignition.

Example of one of the extended crystals:

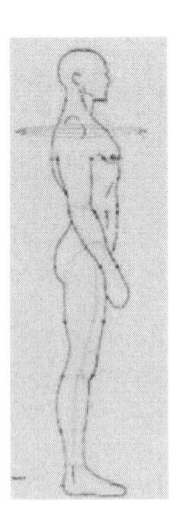

Fire and the " Voladores"

You give the name of "voladores" to every kind of organic or inorganic energy that, as its name says, flies, travels, stirs among planes, worlds, dimensions, etc.

In this chapter we will refer to the "voladores" that take energy away from us like energetic vampires, to voladores "spies" which put themselves in our energetic field without being invited by us, without our permission.

An unbelievable variety of Voladores exists; inside the inorganic ones there are those that are generated in our mind, there are those that live in the astral plane and can follow us up to here in some of our flights, and inside the astral one inorganic voladores that have their own conscience exist.

The common human being or "ordinary" is not conscious of these energies, neither of their acting , only at times he feels excessively tired, very upset, inclusive thoughts near to the death, he can also feel sick and doctors do not find the cause, or he ends with making these thoughts and/or emotions psychosomatic, materializing certain illnesses.

Other times it happens that he feels exultant, full of joy, of strengths and of enthusiasm, and notices that there have not been any changes in his daily life that could produce some radical changes, and he doesn't stop to observe the reason, he only enjoys it and that's it. This last case is when our energy is not poured, it is not absorbed.

We continue without being conscious of the fact that energies dominate our life, of why some have good or bad fortune; we are as leaves in the wind, without having the control of our life and what happens in it.

How many times have you felt an oppression in your leg near the fibula?
How many times have you felt an enormous weight on your back, as if the whole world was on it?
How many times have you felt sharp pains in different parts of your physical body and don't know why?

How many times do you feel that your abdomen inflates to the point to burst?
How many times have you felt as if you had something nailed both in your back, breast, foot or hands?
How many times have you felt that your mind feels like so much to do something but your body doesn't answer to the commands of it?

How many times have you been sick with your stomach, liver, bladder or bowels and you have not eaten or had anything that could have hurt you?
How many times it "seemed" to you that you have seen a shade, something or someone who furtively passed at your side and you have discarded it completely, thinking that it was only your imagination?

How many times have you felt a shiver without having even taken a small gust of cold air?
How many times it "seemed" to you to hear that someone called you by your name and physically nobody did it ?

And many, so many other examples...

For the common human being or "ordinary" the world is only what we are used to perceive, and nevertheless, the world is like the layers of an onion.

In every layer there is a world with its respective beings or energies that live in them, with which we connect "always", either we know it or not.
In each of these worlds there are routes like those that are in our world, there are energetic routes where those energies transfer themselves like we walk on a road.
 We can always find those routes in our own house, there can be one or several ones, but essentially there is always one...and it is the entrance to our physical house.

Other times our house is crossed by various energetic routes through which those energies of those other worlds transfer themselves.
How many times have you felt a strong nausea that lasts just a second, but that shakes you up to the last fibres of your body and there is not any logical explanation for this?

When this happens it is because you were standing still in one of those routes and one of those energies has literally hindered you. It has literally crossed your physical body that is much denser than the thin body of those energies.

Here it is when it becomes necessary to be more conscious of the energy that covers our physical body from which it derives, of our energetic field. We need to be conscious of our energy.

A thing is to talk to grandfather fire in a sacred ceremony around a bonfire, and another different one is to expand the inside fire that lives into us. This inside fire that lives into us lead us first to the second attention and with the daily practice and emphasized ambush to the third attention...do we know in our own flesh that fire that ripples in our inside?...do we know the breath of life that conforms our human energy?.. " have we seen it" and "felt it" blazing in our inside?...have we expanded it inside and around us?

There are many ways to get this awareness, here I will tell in detail the way in which I learned it, the way in which the Spirit, the soul, the universal energy, God, teachers, etc. or as you want to call it taught me and that I share with you.

The fire is the flame of life that lives in the centre of our physical body, some flames ripple tall, others ripple lower... but all of us have this fire of life in our physical body and that maintains us in life.

Our physical body is given by the earth, by our mother earth, to which it will return at our death, I quote: "of dust we are and to dust we will return."

In order that our flame ripples taller, our mother earth helps us blowing great power of life.

How to do this?

Do you remember the exercise of taking roots that we described before?

Well, we will do the same thing, but with certain differences, to be known:

Being still, let's take roots and let's make the fire that lives in the centre of the earth in "shape of" snakes of fire climb our roots, with our will and intention; let's make so that these snakes of fire climb our body up to place themselves in our belly-abdomen. Once in that place and always with our will and intention, let's make so that a snake of fire after the other starts to circularly turn, as soon as we succeed, let's go and give more speed to that turning.

At greater speed, greater will be the power of ignition of the fire, producing the expansion of wider and wider energy of fire, until that energy is amplified in such a way to expand from our inside up to cover us on the outer side of our physical body.

This energy is "our energy." ...it is our "energetic field." At greater energy, greater will be our personal power... At smaller energy, smaller it will be , and according with it, greater or smaller will be our "fortune." With this energy so expanded we are able "to perceive", and to use all the senses that our physical body has: to see, to smell, to touch, to feel and to taste, very beyond what it is considered "normal."

It is as if it was our second "me."... here we enter the second attention, we start to take the first footsteps towards clairvoyance, towards what some call: awake dreaming (ensoñar).

What we see here, feel, listen etc. must not be directed by "rationality.".. what we see is what IS.. '..if we make it pass through the reasoning, we will only get to lose our common sense.

In this experience we must apply what is called ambush, and we must develop the absolute mistrust not to be deceived by our mind neither from the energies that can or cannot stir inside our energetic field; for thus "to know" what they are, from where they originate and what intention they have (the energies that are inside our energetic field).

We cannot believe in their words at once, we must discuss their presence with a fair and brutal mistrust and act.

Descriptive example:

"If a stranger comes in your house without permission, he doesn't ever bring good intentions."

Your energetic field is your house and the "voladores" are the strangers that come in it without your permission. Without your "conscious" permission, because it can happen that we have unconsciously given him permission believing that it was such or that thing, very different from what they really are.

Once the energy of fire is already expanded out of your physical body, first we must spy our body and observe with great attention and mistrust if we have "something" glued or also that wants to enter inside us. In this part we will apply our fierce reasoning. Once we know what, from where and why it is there, we will use the power of our fire through our will (mind) to get it away from there. It can happen that at times a battle happens among that energy and us, which we must win.

The fire can be used through our mental power or our physical qualities of personal defence, always influenced by the fire.

Once by now we are sure that our body is free from the "voladores", let's expand our energy of fire with our will and intention for the whole place where we are, until it touches the four walls, floor and ceiling; and we return to spy and to discuss.

Energy doesn't know distances, it can expand up to where we would or we could, according to the accumulation of personal power. At greater daily practice, greater that power will be.

> Nadie es más que nadie...
> Aún en los grandes sabios el ego muestra su presencia...
> Aún en los grandes maestros, la importancia personal dice a veces "presente"...

Nobody is more than anybody..
Also in great wise men the ego shows its presence...
Also in great teachers, personal importance says at times "present.".

Strengthening our character...

The human beings with a lot of energy usually have a strong character or a bad character...

very different things!!!

The strong character speaks of an iron will...the bad character speaks of the lack of temperance of that will...of lack of balance...

The human being of strong character has a direct will and has been strengthened from fire and from water as the blacksmith with its club...

In this human being the conscious love lives...he can say: NO or YES...and this no or yes, will be full of love...

If we don't strengthen our character in fire and in water...when we wake up in the sea of the conscience, we will lose ourselves there...

By now awaken in the sea that is our conscience...and having received the first beams of light...we can remain blind and prisoners of our mind...

Confusing vision with imagination...and in this blindness we create a chaos in which we dip and we submerge those who believe in us...

As once I have learned: "You need the same humility to know and accept our shade as to know and accept our light...thus the shades illuminate themselves and the light doesn't blind us..."

This humility allows us to strengthen our character...and not to fall in mental digressions...

Once strengthened our character...our will is ready to serve us as the most sublime tool of our soul...

And there will not be anything that we cannot succeed in getting...without giving importance to what the others say...neither the experiences of others...we can go and get everything our soul desires...

Evolution is part of this...to go beyond...with humility as heart...

The rolling shutters of dream (ensueño)

When we start to lucid dream (ensoñar) we must know that there are different rolling shutters to cross, it depends on the evolution of every soul. The first rolling shutters come in number of eight (8), which we will cross one by one; we cannot see them before time, we are allowed to see the first one, after having crossed it and done our task in it, we will be shown the second one and so forth up to reach the eighth rolling shutter.

Later and with the due process of incarnation (application in the daily life of each of us of what we have learned there), the second line of rolling shutters of dream will come, that is not anything else than the unification of the eight (8) first unified rolling shutters in couple, therefore the second line of rolling shutters towards dreaming(ensoñar) is composed of four (4) rolling shutters, which, as the first line, we will go experimenting one by one.

 Once finished this second line of rolling shutters of dream and with the due process of application in the daily life of each one (incarnation) of what we have learned there, in front of us the next to last line of the rolling shutters of dream opens.

Up to here we can count that in two (2) sections we have crossed twelve (12) rolling shutters of the dream, to which the process arrives to unify them in only one rolling shutter of dream, the number thirteen (13). At this point we will already have succeeded in visiting many worlds, remembering who we were, why we came to this world and for what purpose; we will have succeeded in learning everything all the teachers, that live in all the worlds, planes, dimensions, have to teach us, and we will be able to bring that knowledge to this world for us, who will have turned it into wisdom applying it (embody it).

Here we reach the last section of the rolling shutters of dream, that which will bring us to the total freedom, this last line comes in number of: "without-calculation".

What each one experiments in every rolling shutter of the dream will be limited to our own ability to keep our mind silent (to enter the lucid dream with direction and intention but without expecting anything in "particular", without "conditioning" what we must experiment and learn there).

In the dream the use of rationality only removes from us the opportunity to learn and to experiment the endless possibilities that the universe puts at our disposal as the perceivers we are, and it puts us in front of the danger to lose ourselves inside our own mind, which tends always "to imagine", "to suppose", "to believe" that it is real what is not.

Changing the point of joint (angle) as you like.

A lot of people do it in an unconscious way or they already know how to do it, but for who has not succeeded yet:

The ideal thing is starting to practise the awake (lucid) dream, and from this place change the point of joint (angle). What is the point of joint (angle)? It is simply where we put our attention, if we were perceiving a sequence of images in a determined scenery, we can decide inside the dream to change our perception towards another situation, place, etc.

Means that help us to enter the lucid dream:

- To walk letting our mind flow or trying "to know" something in particular.
-To succeed in totally keeping our mind silent.
-To close our eyes, take any thought of the many that sail in our mind, and "follow" its course up to reach its end.
-To focus our sight on any point, that is in the air, on a wall, in the small void of a smaller rock measured on our hand, in a photo and "let ourselves be carried", not checking the situation, but yes, being very careful to what we see and to what happens and if we don't want to keep on perceiving what

happens there, simply we can change the point of attention, we can move the point of angling.

With a constant practice of this exercise and when we already have a thin and light handling of the technique, we can start to practise the moving of the point of angling at our will inside the dream, succeeding in this way in passing from a common dream to an "ensueño" and from this to another dream.

For this reason we must already go to bed with the firm intention "to wake up " inside the dream to realize that we are lucid dreaming (ensoñar) and to take the decisions that we would like to take. When we fall asleep, besides the firm intention, we must also give a "direction" to our dream: where do we want to wake up inside the dream? Who do we want to lucid dream with?

As the proverb says: " practice makes the monk", practice without hurry but without breaks and the objective will always be reached.

Ensoñar (lucid dreaming) without lying in ambush is like putting ourselves in a battleground without shields and without weapons. Lucid dreaming and lying in ambush must go constantly together taken by the hand...one must not act without the other.

When we enter the dream we must spy with absolute mistrust everything we see, we feel, we touch for knowing if in reality it is such as we are seeing it, feeling it; we must discuss ourselves and "that" with ferocity, if it is real or it is an image that doesn't show what really is. We must always distrust, mistrust is the most important weapon of an "ensoñador" (dreamer), in every field, awake or asleep.

Lucid dreaming without lying in ambush only puts us without shields in the

battleground...

Whispers of the Spirit...

I looked through the window
 That starry night,
  When a tinkling caught My attention...
 and I remained there,
  As frozen in time.

That afternoon in autumn
Found Me sat on the
Bench of the garden,
the tormenting wind
made the leaves dance
When an almost
Imperceptible movement
in the cup of a Tree,
caught my attention
And I remained there...as frozen
In time.

I quietly walked on the beach
Leaving that the foamy waves bathed
My feet, when a dwarfish shine
On the waters caught my attention...
And I remained there, as frozen in time.

It was the dawn already when
I Reached the top of that mountainous chain and
Decided to give my legs some rest
I took a seat, when a sound just audible
Caught my attention...and I remained there,
 As frozen in time.

How many times does it happen to us and do we remain long minutes in silence without thinking about anything?

>	Many times!...but

what happens in that loop of time?

We do not remember it!!

The Universe speaks to us in thousands of ways, but few times we have the necessary strength "to keep" those "conversations" in our conscious memory. And as the trunk of memories, our unconsciousness stores them, leaving that conversation, that learning in forgetfulness...

The whole wisdom of the Universe is inside us, it is only necessary to open the doors, to remove the cobwebs, to clean the path towards our unconsciousness and to bring to light one by one our forgotten memories by that trunk.

Every time that we remain "as" frozen in time, it is because we are in front of the doors of the second attention, if we spy, we can enter to awake lucid dreaming... how many times has it happened to us?

The idea is that of incorporating lucid dreaming, lying in ambush and recapitulating the lived thing in the dream as a daily practice... you take knowledge and you don't lose energy.

The woman or the man nagual and the attentions

The "naguales" and clairvoyants of ancient times reached certain attentions, and on them there is a lot of writing: Carlos Castaneda with his various books and the teachings of Don Juan Mattus, Domingo Delgado Solórzano with the book "the nagual of 5 points." All these left us a legacy thanks to which we can learn and/or understand many of our experiences, but if we are stagnant in our footsteps and we don't transcend them we will remain entangled in the past.

Going far beyond the teachers

In all the philosophies that are in this world...in all the planes and dimensions there are teachers who have "something" to teach us, and from whom we can learn.

But in turn, the paradigm exists that in exchange for their teaching, and in an unconscious way for us, they entangle us in their world...
"we get married" with him / them, remaining there for indefinite time; instead once we have taken the knowledge that is there for each of us..."letting go" everything with endless gratitude and going on...without "stagnating"...without " getting married"...

We boast about some acquired knowledge and there we succumb, losing our freedom....

Is there spiritual "nepotism"?... is there energetic nepotism?....yes...there is...

"as it is above so it is below" an old wise man said...

We open our mind...we let go all that we have learned...and we go on and more...and we return to let go...once and another one...

The great teachers of all the philosophies, planes and dimensions don't want our total freedom....

And this happens because we allow it...nobody more than ourselves...

Everything is for transcending, using, bringing to our mankind and applying it to the same one, it is the only way to evolve. If we have experiences and we don't understand them and we don't look for the way to apply them to our humanity we will live separated in two worlds, in two roads: the "tonal" (material) and the "nahual" (energetic and spiritual).

The first attention

It is that in which we move in our day to day life; here ambush starts, but that ambush is done with total alert every second of our days; to correctly do it we must apply it in both the directions: towards our inside and towards our outside at the same time. It is useless to spy what or who comes into contact with our vital energetic field or with our body of dream if at the same time we don't spy ourselves to discover, to know and to eradicate our personal importance, the struggles of power that develop in our inside; since it is the only battleground where they develop.

Attaining the almost automatic practice of ambush takes us a certain time in constancy and discipline.

Let's ask ourselves questions like: What in me makes me irritate in front of such situation, words or gestures of the other? - What in me makes me feel less or more in comparison with others? - What in me makes me reveal, complain, distress, keep silent what I don't dare to say?
 What in me makes me fear not to get this or that? - What in me makes me fear the abandonment of my dear ones? What in me makes me "need" to be in company and to fear loneliness? Which beliefs in me makes me consider this one a failure and that a success?

Discussing with ourselves of this and much more in the mental silence and answering us with absolute sincerity towards ourselves, understanding that ALL passes through and inside us and not through the others will conduct us to the gradual liberation from inherited and/or self-imposed chains with the logical consequence of energy increasing (personal power); that sincerity is the true humility of the warrior.

The practice of ambush doesn't ask for extra time that we must steal to our daily matters, we must develop it at the same time as doing every thing during our day.

Spying our thoughts, our reactions, before and after having expressed them, our desires, our emotions, spying our actions and what we don't do and why we don't do it.

This is the beginning of the path towards knowledge.

The second attention

Here we start to develop the ability to see beyond what our physical eyes can see, to understand that there are other worlds apart of which we know and that those worlds are just here, in front of our noses.

The majority of the people distrusts what they see, they attribute it to their imagination, to a momentary madness or to games done by their mind. It is here where ambush is the best tool on which we count for establishing if what we see or we experiment awake or asleep is "real." This is the principle of the dream being awake. If we observe with care, absolute alert, we will be able to experiment "as if" we were inside a film, in which we will discover that we can change the course of it or continue it; if inside that "film" we interact, we are moving the point of angling, that we had always fixed in the ordinary reality, at our will towards other realities.

It is required the union of all the realities...to find the point where all the realities meet and influence us in a way or in another one.

Lucid dreaming awake we need fundamental questions besides the ambush and it deals with the hunting of knowledge and its way of applying it to our humanity, to our physical body and from this application we must act in our social world with this acquired knowledge, transformed by now into personal wisdom:

1- How can I apply this to my humanity?
2- What is the practical way to do it?
3 - what is it for?
4 - how can I bring it to words?
5 - how can I share this knowledge with others?

We can contemporarily act in various realities.. contemporarily being in various planes of conscience and interacting in almost all of them "contemporarily."

Here we start to chase knowledge giving a hand to ambush and dream.

If you spy another one and you don't spy yourself why you are spying another one, what drives you to spy him, you will never know the complete whole of ambush.

If our practice is led with constancy and discipline, we will arrive to live in a continuous way in the second attention so as to conscious lucid dream while being asleep.

Like the old nagual said, it is a job of 24 hours, second by second, but for this we must be here and now, in the present, in this second, in this sacred instant. In the moment when we go out of the present, we already stop being in the second attention and we return to be as leaves in the wind manipulated by our emotions that derive from our thoughts, which live in the past or in the future.

To go into lucid dreaming intention and direction are required, without this there is no dream (ensueño).

It is as we want to go out on the road and do not know where we want to go and for what reason.

The more we feed and we keep swaying our tall inside fire, the more we will have power and better we will lucid dream and we will spy, all equally: men as women.

In these present times it is necessary to debunk the fact that only women have easiness in lucid dreaming, the men that hold their inside fire high reach the same knowledge, the same conscience, the same ability of knowledge of any woman.

They do not "need" to feed from women in this sense...they can succeed by themselves, this grants them a liberty that they didn't have before.

For respect towards men and women this change of paradigm is required. This way you avoid to fall in the practices of the old school where men reached only a certain conscience or knowledge through the physical sexual practice with women.

The world is a predator, yes, but there are ways and ways to feed oneself; we are naturally predators, we feed of the conscience and energy of the plants and fruits that we eat, we feed of the conscience and energy of the animals that we eat, it is not necessary to feed of the conscience and energy of another human being.

We all equally can produce that energy and conscience in ourselves through the inside fire.

In the measure in which we stay more and more time in the second attention and we dare to put the lived things, remembered and learned there, into practice in our humanity, we will go and cross one by one every plane of every dimension. Changing in this way, we go to change our reality and what before struck us, by now it does no more, without caring if the society in which we live and of which we are part changes or not.

The third attention

To go into this attention we need a certain "death", a certain delivery of everything we are humanly to the forces that direct us, both celestial and terrestrial.

For this reason the person approaches to mother earth, makes his/her mind keep silent, put oneself in the present, in the here and now, and feels the mighty energy of the earth and compares with it... How does he/she feel in the comparison?... What feelings are born in his/her heart towards mother earth?... Then he observes the star-populated sky and its immensity and feels its mighty energy and compares with it... How does he/she feel in the comparison?... What feelings are born in his/her heart towards that mighty immensity?

Let the person observe the kinetic energy of the trees, of the plants that surround him/her and contemporarily feel in his/her own flesh that he/she perceives the wonder of life, the wonder to be alive, to be a part of all that. Overwhelmed by these feelings and understanding from his/her own experience how small we are in front of those immensities, and thankful to be a part of the same, we deliver everything we are humanly to the forces that direct us, we direct our most sincere and humble words to them, we deliver our thoughts and emotions, successes and mistakes, our physical body, our desires and our will, our physical life and by now empty of everything we perceive with our closed eyes whatever human being that passes nearby...How do you perceive him?.. What is the energy living in him like? Do you perceive any energy rippling inside? Where do you place it?

This is the kingdom of God and once gone into it we can perceive everything as he does and feel as he feels... God is not that gentleman with a white beard that everyone adores, he is energy of life in this world, God lives in the earth and in everything existing in it, either we perceive it or not.

And yes, humanly we are at his image and similarity, full fire of life, mighty strength of love and fullness.

The fourth attention

The fourth attention is more complex than the preceding ones, it requires much more ambush, a subtler and deeper ambush on oneself. You are asked for a total lack of fear of death, but at the same time of a total acceptance of what we are, and this not only asks for an enormous amount of honesty but of bravery.

There is a sentence that says: "The whole lot is known through its parts."

To enter the fourth attention we must dismember us energetically speaking. To realize this, we will do it from the second attention and we will use ambush as a sublime mean.

Remember that to live in the second attention the only way is to be here and now.

One of the many ways:

Let's take the name of any person as example: Sarah

a- Sarah decides to spy herself...her thoughts, which they are, where they come from, where they go towards, what is the destination. To do this Sarah does it without any judgments, criticisms neither justifications towards herself, what it is: IS.

But: Who spies this Sarah ? Another part of Sarah that spies the Sarah who thinks.. and it spies her up to know and to understand how and why her mind is how it is. Which part of Sarah is this second Sarah?...her mental part, her emotional part, her physical part, her spiritual part?... Which one?

b- If it exists a Sarah that spies the Sarah who thinks, is it because it exists a third part of Sarah that spies the second one; what is this third part of Sarah?
c- Ambush after ambush, layer behind layer, up to know what each of our parts are like, independently if we like them or not.

What is our emotional body like? What is our mental body like? What is our physical body like and what is its state like? How do we perceive each of these?

Ambush and still ambush up to that we can perceive contemporarily and from our spirit the shape and composition of the other three bodies "separated" and we will understand the why of the state of each one and on which we must work later.
Once we perceive all of our separate parts we will feel a peace and an indescribable serenity and we won't want to go out of that state; as well as we will discover that a part or more of the WHOLE LOT that conforms us is not of our taste, on the contrary, we won't like to return to integrate a lot of it under any aspect.

In this state and still without integrating all of our parts again, we enter the fourth attention, so, separated we can stay three (3) days neither one minute more if we don't want to physically die. Already in the fourth attention we will be in ambush and we will chase knowledge.

The normal thing in these states is that the separated physical body almost cannot stir, to be in a state of total disconnection of its parts, but contemporarily we can enjoy a marvellous state. It is of extreme importance that before the three days are spent we again gather all of our parts, inclusive those that we despise or we fear, if we want to return from the fourth attention to this plane.

Once we have performed this process it will be less complex for us to enter and to go out of the fourth attention every time we like "to bring" knowledge.

Already in the fourth attention our energetic double, or the shade that goes out of the head to every nagual that has embodied those energies, will be "grown up", if the expression fits, enormously, we will perceive it as a giant of many meters high aside our physical body.

The fifth attention

As soon as we evolve it would seem that everything becomes more complicated, but you can resolve it remaining in the "present", in this way fears, doubts, etc. do not strike us and don't bend us.

To the fifth attention we enter with our double (shade of the nagual) and our vital energy (snake of fire) towards the part of the external interstice of Black Eagle; in this interstice a translucent grey energy lives where you will find four eagles still opaque, still grabbed to their snakes of fire and you will put yourself together with them, deciding whether letting go your snake of fire or not.

Taken the decision to free your snake of fire you will do it just there, it is the payment that Black Eagle asks you in exchange for letting you go towards freedom with the body and everything.

When you succeed in this, you can return to this reality without physically dying; as everything is a process, after some days (in all the human beings time is something relative) you will fly again to the fifth attention by now only with your energetic double (shade of the nagual) and, like the sun at the dawn, you will illuminate the four eagles that are waiting there with your own energy; these will free at their turn their respective snakes and will join to your flight back to mother earth, transformed into your wings, two at every side, united to two forming a wing at every side of your nagual energy, by now completed your double in nagual of five points.

To be continued....

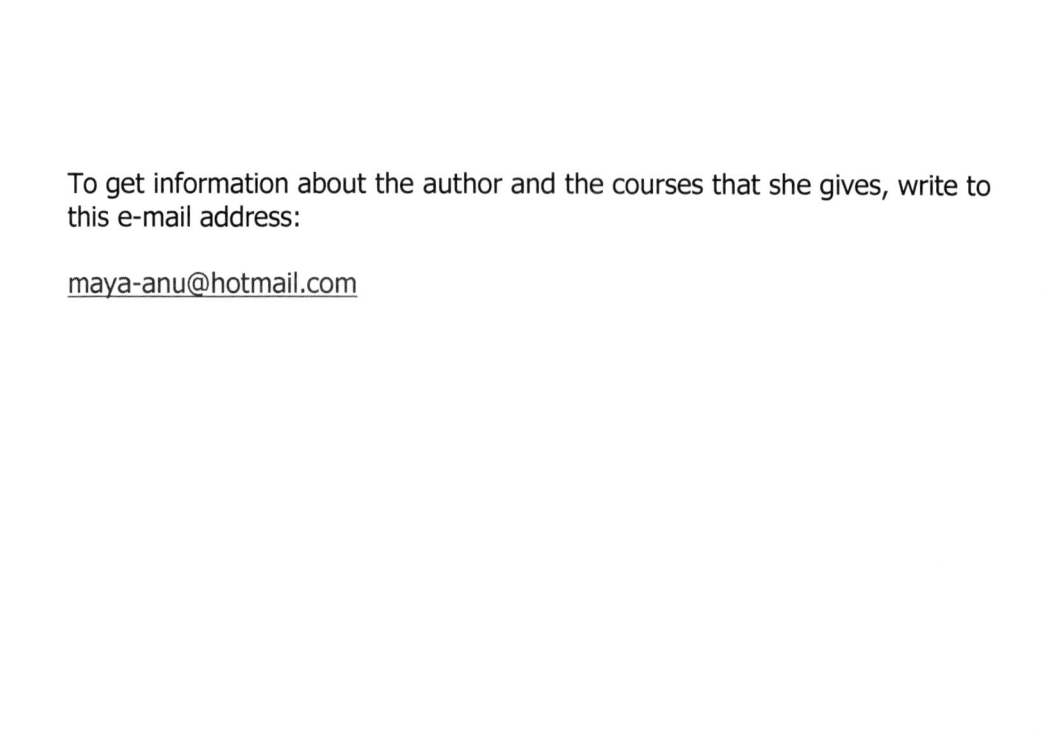

To get information about the author and the courses that she gives, write to this e-mail address:

maya-anu@hotmail.com

Printed in Great Britain
by Amazon